STILL ANGELA

JENNY KEMP

CURRENCY PRESS
The performing arts publisher

First published in 2002
by Currency Press Pty Ltd,
PO Box 2287, Strawberry Hills, NSW, 2012, Australia
enquiries@currency.com.au
www.currency.com.au

in association with Playbox Theatre, Melbourne

This revised edition published 2005

Reprinted in 2010, 2011, 2012, 2015, 2022

Typeset by Dean Nottle.

Currency Press acknowledges the Traditional Owners of the Country on which we live and work. We pay our respects to all Aboriginal and Torres Strait Islander Elders, past and present.

A catalogue record for this book is available from the National Library of Australia

Contents

DESERT QUOTES

Extracts from *The Australian Desert* reprinted by kind permission of the publisher, Reed Education Australia.

Text from 'The Songlines' by Bruce Chatwin—desert facts written by Patrick Thaiday.
(www.oneworldmagazine.org/focus/deserts/watext.htm)

Jenny Kemp website: http://www.blacksequin.com/

'After all what happens to the self is arbitrary; it is only by following, interpreting, naming the affronts to the sensibility, living them over again, that the self establishes control over them.'

'sit still sit still the lively understandable
spirit said,
still, still,
so that it can be completely the
now.'

'… at the most primordial level of sensuous, bodily experience, we find ourselves in an expressive, gesturing landscape, in a world that speaks.'

'Consider a spider weaving its web… Whatever the "instructions"… are enfolded within the living genome, they can hardly predict the specifics of the microterrain within which the spider may find itself at any particular moment… They could hardly have determined in advance the exact distances between the cave wall and the branch that the spider is now employing as an anchorage point for her current web, or the exact strength of the monsoon rains that make web-spinning a bit more difficult on this evening…'

CHARACTERS

ANGELA 1, late 20s.

ANGELA 2, early 30s.

ANGELA 3, 40 years old.

THE GIRL, a younger Angela. This character represents Angela at six years old, but to be played by a mature dancer/actor. The voice of the girl should be spoken by Angela 1.

JACK, Angela's boyfriend, mid 30s.

DONALD, a man on the train (played by the same actor as Otto).

OTTO, early 40s.

THE MOTHER, Angela's mother, 40 years old (the same age as Angela 3). Played with yellow face or realistic mask, except for in the 'Down the Throat' scene. This role may be played by a dancer/actor. However the voice of the mother may be best as a voice-over.

THE FATHER, Angela's father (played by same actor as Otto). With glasses and hat. A peripheral presence in Section One and in the desert domestic sequence.

STEWARD, a steward on the desert train (played by the same actor as Otto). He is always a little unreadable.

WAITER, on the train / dining car (played by the same actor as Jack).

THE CHARACTERS AT THE FANCY DRESS PARTY

ANGELA 1, a man's suit, but strips to bra and trousers.

ANGELA 2, nurse's outfit with a bird feather on her cap.

ANGELA 3, Angela's blue dress with a tumbleweed hat.

GIRL, schoolgirl with an adult wig of hair, and adult shoes.

MOTHER, mother's dress and very long black wig.

JACK, Hermes. Waiter's uniform, now white with gold buttons and cap with wings on his heels.

OTTO, a Shakespearean grave digger.

A NOTE ON THE FOUR ANGELAS

The play examines Angela during a period of transition. As a theatrical device the character of Angela is played by four actors.

We have within ourselves, at any moment, our past and the potential for our future. It is as if the potential for any of these Angelas is present and possible, at any moment.

It is intended that the audience can interpret this dynamic in a number of ways and that various narratives are possible.

Film, music/sound and choreography should play key roles in building the form of this work.

Still Angela was first produced by Playbox Theatre at The C.U.B. Malthouse, Melbourne, on 10 April 2002 with the following cast:

> Natasha Herbert
> Felicity MacDonald
> Margaret Mills
> Mark Minchinton
> Lucy Taylor
> Ros Warby
> Simon Wilton

Director, Jenny Kemp
Choreography, Helen Herbertson
Composition, Elizabeth Drake
Design, Jacqueline Everitt
Lighting Design, David Murray
Film, Ben Speth
Script Consultancy, Mark Minchinton

To Helen Kemp

PROLOGUE: ANGELA SITTING / THE KITCHEN

ANGELA 3 *is seen sitting alone in a small square of light on the block which is not yet fully revealed. She is speaking. During the speech we switch to see* ANGELA 1. *As we switch she seamlessly takes over the speech. Finally we switch to* ANGELA 2, *who at first is silent as* ANGELA 1*'s voice continues, then speaks. Eventually we see all three Angelas at the same time.*

ANGELA 3: A kitchen, a kitchen sink, a window, a clothes line out the window, a chair on which I sit. A small table. Lino under the chair, checks, an ordered type of lino. Pink shiny walls. Flesh pink. A kettle, a stove, a few saucepans, a bench, a chopping board. All these things to keep me going. Cups, saucers, knives and forks. A fridge, frozen food, ice blocks, Alaska in my fridge, mini Alaska. A broom, a blowfly, a back door.

> *Slight pause.*

Then all the other things that later you have to get. Rubber gloves, a scouring pad, Ajax, a brush and pan, a peddle bin, a wettex. Oh and then some glasses for wine. A bottle opener, a tin opener.

> ANGELA 1 *begins to speak under* ANGELA 3.

And the things for the kitchen that I keep in the laundry, the mop, the bucket, the floor cleaner, the garbage bin, compost bucket.

> *Slight pause.*

It's so complicated.

ANGELA 1: And then I have to go to the market and get food and toiletries. I look into the cupboard and see what has run out. I write a list, then get the basket and set off. I usually lose the note. And I always forget a key item. And the laundry is there for the washing. Then when I step outside I see the garden is dry. I must water the garden, dig the garden, weed the garden, prune the trees. Get the letters in, then read the letters, answer the letters, the bills, the invitations, and all the letters asking for help or money. I must decide exactly what to do about them, which one to give to.

ANGELA 2 *begins to speak under* ANGELA 1.

What if I don't, what does it mean? That I'm mean spirited? Then I go to bed, but before I go, I must clean my teeth, go to the toilet and turn off the light.

ANGELA 2: And that's all nothing to do with work, work is on top of all that. Eating and work. And then there's play, pleasure, recreation, going out. Keeping up with relationships, friends.

Stop thinking, thinking doesn't help.

Slight pause.

There's a spider on the wall, in the corner. It must have come in through the window. It's come in because it rained last night. It's so still, it could be dead. It must be waiting for something or resting.

The trees are moving. The trees are green. It's an evergreen, the wind is moving the branches. It's from the north, it's carried you away, off to nowhere, off to somewhere. You've disappeared.

Slight pause.

The spider is still still, in the middle of its pattern. It lives in a complex pattern which came out of its body, its home, which traps its food for it.

To be spoken by ANGELA 3. ANGELA 1 *and* 2 *also speak the sections underlined.*

ANGELA 3: She knew that the sandwich was inside her. The earth, the bushes, the trees all have their sandwiches 'just as I do', she said to herself, 'just as I do.' There was something to discover about time, it was as if the sandwich, the bushes, the trees, the earth, were all getting on with something and she just wasn't quite getting it. Something important was eluding her. She could discover what if she remained quite still she felt.

The trees are drinking all the time internally, up out of the earth, up the trunk and into the leaves, yet I cannot see it, I know, but I cannot see it.

SECTION ONE: ANGELA SITTING / MEMORY

In the space there are three lit corridors (about 3.5 meters long and half a meter wide), one behind the other. There is a small unlit corridor between each one. There is one chair somewhere in the corridors. The three adult ANGELAS, JACK, *the* MOTHER *and the* FATHER *are on stage in the corridors. Throughout this section the characters work within the corridors (sometimes along the unlit corridors). Whenever one changes direction the others also change direction, so at times it is as if the corridors run upstage, and at times across the stage. The characters move within the parameters of stillness to movement, sometimes sitting, in a kind of rhythmic dance or game. The* MOTHER *and* FATHER *are present yet more peripheral than the others.*

This sequence is Angela's process of sorting, sifting, remembering. It should depend on a complex pattern of spatial dynamics. Although the scenes between Angela 1 and Jack are realistic, no props are used, and any gestures or actions used by the actors should be minimal, precise yet simplified, they are the essence of something remembered. The internal rhythm of Angela 3 is established here. As she sits (or at times moves) she travels internally, her memories and emotions bounce, jostle and nudge at her for attention. The action should be rhythmic, as if Angela inhabits areas as she gives them focus. Or alternately her thoughts or memories erupt or appear with a volition of their own.

ANGELA *has stopped because she cannot go on. Eventually the next action occurs: 'to go to the desert'.*

JACK AND ANGELA IN THE KITCHEN / LOST KEYS

Movement on the corridors begins.

ANGELA 1: [*with real urgency as she's so late*] Where're my keys! I can't see them anywhere!

    JACK *gestures that he doesn't know, she keeps hunting.*

Shit! Who left all this stuff here?!

JACK: Actually. You. Tea.

ANGELA 1: Oww! I've burnt my tongue!

JACK: Sorry about that.

> ANGELA 1 *looks at her watch.*

ANGELA 1: I'm late! God I'm going to be so late!

> JACK *stamps on ants, looks under his shoe.*

JACK: Shit. Ants.

ANGELA 1: Egh? Oh.

> *She sees the keys on the floor, grabs them.*

Have to go! 'Bye!

> *She kisses* JACK *and runs.*

Don't forget you're supposed to pick me up after work!

> *She stops—it is* ANGELA 3*'s voice which stops her.*

TRAVELLING DOWN HER CHILDHOOD GARDEN PATH / THE BACKYARD

ANGELA 3: Don't step on the lines. Snakes in the concrete.

> *Pause.*

Behind me the side gate. To my right the wall of the house. The window. The gully trap. The path...

> *She stops.*

JACK AND ANGELA IN THE KITCHEN / WASHING DISHES

ANGELA 1 *is very pre-menstrual. She has dropped something or hurt herself.*

ANGELA 1: [*exploding*] Shit!

JACK: Break something?

ANGELA 1: [*irritated*] How many times this week have you done the dishes?

JACK: I did them on Sunday.

ANGELA 1: Well it's Thursday now!

> JACK *goes to her then he stops.*

JACK: You should have said something.

ANGELA 1: I don't like the feeling in my body.

> *Pause.*

JACK: I'm sorry. [*Trying to lighten things up*] I do nice things to your body too.

> *She grins a little despite herself.*

Didn't we have a nice time last night?

ANGELA 1: It's not a joke!

JACK: Angel?

> *Pause.*

ANGELA 2: I'm not an angel, Jack.

ANGELA SITTING / THE SPIDER

ANGELA 3: The spider is so still it could be dead.

> *Pause.*

I'd love a cigarette.

JACK AND ANGELA IN THE KITCHEN / LAMB'S FRY AND BACON

JACK *chases* ANGELA 1. *They dodge each other and giggle. They continue the game throughout the scene.*

ANGELA 1: You look sweet and smooth, with your whiskers far back inside your skin.

JACK: My bristles hidden, my fur combed flat.

> ANGELA *is humming. She dances with him.*

ANGELA 1: [*while dancing or dodging with energy*] Do you remember when we met, Jack?! You cooked me a beautiful dinner!!

> JACK *is still playing.*

JACK: Did I?!

ANGELA 1: Lamb's fry and bacon!

JACK: Did you like that?!

ANGELA 1: Yes!

JACK: Through your stomach to your heart!

> *She does a gyrating movement against him.*

ANGELA 1: Yes!!

JACK: I hope you're not masturbating on me!

> *She stops dancing. She pulls back and stares at him, he remains still.*

I'm joking, I'm joking. Come on. It was sexy.

ANGELA THE BAT

ANGELA 3: So Angela and the bat what is the connection?

Is Angela's sitting a blind act?
Is Angela a bat?
A creature of the night, of darkness, of stillness?
Has Angela stopped because she was about to crash?
But this does not mean that Angela is not travelling,
Angela is on the hunt for the grit inside her shell,
Angela is aging, she is at a crucial age, travelling through a particular passage.

JACK AND ANGELA IN THE KITCHEN / ANTS

ANGELA *is very late for work again.*

JACK: Ants! Everywhere! Shit! You left out the lamb.

ANGELA 1: I know, I know.

JACK: All right, I'm just reminding you. Do you know where my singlet is?

ANGELA 1: It's in a pile on the floor.

JACK: I slept like a log. Am I taking the car today or you?

ANGELA 1: Me!

JACK: Could you give me a lift in?

ANGELA 1: Okay.

She starts to go.

Hurry up!

Pause.

ANGELA SITTING / JUST A BLOWFLY AND ME

ANGELA 3: Nothing else, just a blowfly and me.

I can hear a TV in the distance, some people talking. I can hear the wind. I can hear nothing, nothing at all.

I can't hear you Jack you don't have any sound, any presence, as if you were creeping along the pavement with bare feet, trying to trick me.

It's just a wall, with a tiny crack, inside it's dark, it's crumbled away.

Behind the crack is bricks and mortar. Behind the wall outside, a backyard.

It's still raining. Everything will be wet. Don't throw out the baby with the bath water said my mother.

Short pause.

What baby? [*Quietly*] She's disappeared. Like one of those people inside a child's wardrobe. When you open the door nothing. You're walking around my head. You're a monster of love now. I'll have to get a gun or knife and kill you off.

The orange blossom is blooming, it's collapsing onto the ground… it's so ripe.

JACK AND ANGELA IN THE KITCHEN / GAME OF CHESS

ANGELA 1: [*calling out*] I'm cleaning up. Then I'm going to make an old-fashioned sandwich with tomato and onion, and sit down and have it.

JACK: Yep. Yep. Yep. Terrific! I'll get the stuff from the fridge! And there's a bit of wine left.

ANGELA 1: It's going to pour.

Slight pause then JACK *appears.*

JACK: Hey, guess what I bought?
ANGELA 1: What?
JACK: Chess. Want a game?
ANGELA 1: Now?
JACK: Yes. With the sandwich.
ANGELA 1: But I haven't played for years.
JACK: You'll remember.

> ANGELA 1 *thinks it's a good idea.*

ANGELA 1: Okay.

TRAVELLING DOWN HER CHILDHOOD GARDEN PATH / THE BACKYARD

ANGELA 1 *is practising a dance step quietly, trying to remember how it goes.*

ANGELA 3: One step at a time…

> *Slight pause.*

Hot day. Mirage on the path.

JACK AND ANGELA IN THE KITCHEN / THE CHA CHA CHA

ANGELA 1 *practises a dance step—she can't quite get it.* JACK *is playful.* ANGELA 1 *keeps dodging and practising.* JACK *and* ANGELA 1 *dodge each other, he makes her laugh.*

ANGELA 1: Step step step, step step. One two… stops three, one two…

> JACK *is still playing.*

JACK: What's that?
ANGELA 1: One two, one… How did it go? One two.

> ANGELA 1 *is getting tired. She stops, her mood shifting.*

I'm going to get a glass of water.
JACK: What about going out tonight?
ANGELA 1: You go.
JACK: Very funny.
ANGELA 1: I've worked a ten-hour day.

JACK AND ANGELA IN THE KITCHEN / THE GAME OF CHESS

ANGELA 2: The pawn is a soldier, he's a dog's body. He goes forward one step at a time. The horse two forward and one to the side. The horse can jump. I like the horse. It can do what the others can't. They look squashed like they will crash into each other if they are not careful. They are at war. The rules are. There's the bishop, he travels sideways, never straight ahead. The castle is solid and round, where they all go to sleep. It's magic because it can move, only in straight lines though. The king stands in the centre with the queen. He can hardly move at all, just one step at a time, but he's very important, no one comes near him because if they do he imprisons them immediately. Everyone is trying to trick the king. Everyone is scared when the queen is nearby because she can take in all sorts of ways.

ANGELA 3: Behind the door something tiny like a stab wound.

JACK AND ANGELA IN THE KITCHEN / I'M LONELY

JACK *stamps on some ants. The minute* ANGELA *hears the bang—she wants something new to happen and is deciding to go out.*

JACK: Did we take anything out of the freezer for dinner?

ANGELA 1: I didn't.

JACK: Should have left the fish out.

> *He squashes ants, looks under his boot.*

Are there any eggs?

ANGELA 1: No.

JACK: Right.

> *Pause.*

Why didn't you dance with me last night?

ANGELA 1: You were occupied.

JACK: I sound like a toilet.

ANGELA 1: Well that is what you were.

Pause.

JACK: You appeared to have a good time for yourself.

Pause.

ANGELA 2: I'm lonely, Jack.

JACK: [*not defensively*] Well I'm not.

ANGELA 1: No. Well how is that?

JACK: I'm not good company.

ANGELA 2: It's not like that.

JACK: Oh.

ANGELA 1 *is changing her mind about going out.*

ANGELA 1: I'm going to bed. I'm going to read my book. Then I'm going to sleep.

JACK: I'm glad you told me all that.

ANGELA AND THE BAT NO. 2

ANGELA 3: Is Angela sleeping with her eyes open? In a sense hanging upside down? Has her radar told her that any movement in any direction is dangerous…?

JACK AND ANGELA IN THE KITCHEN / ANGELA TELLS HER DECIMATED HOUSE AND BABY DREAM

ANGELA 1 *stands in sexy underwear holding her dress.*

ANGELA 1: I came home and everything was decimated. The mattresses cut open, the phone cut open, the furniture upside down. Everything was stripped, gutted.

She stops and stares at him.

Are you listening, at all?!

JACK *stops eating for a moment.*

JACK: I'm listening.

He keeps eating but more slowly and watching her.

ANGELA 1: Anyway, then I saw a baby lying on a little shelf which was its bed. I went up and realised if it rolled over in its sleep it would fall.

And I noticed its feet were over the end of the shelf, it was too big for the shelf. I took hold of its feet but I had the feeling it wasn't really my baby to look after but someone else's.

JACK nods. He stops eating for a moment.

JACK: Perhaps it's you.
ANGELA 1: Perhaps it's you.

He starts eating again. She stares at him. Pause.

Why do you just keep stuffing yourself with cornflakes!?

JACK stops and looks at her.

JACK: I'm hungry.

Pause.

I didn't have any dinner last night.

Pause, then not unkindly.

You told me your dream before.

He looks at her in her underwear, realising what she may be intending.

Do you want to have sex?

She did but now she's offended.

ANGELA 1: Not at the moment. I'm going to get dressed and go out.
JACK: With that underwear under your clothes?
ANGELA 1: I thought I would.
JACK: Any particular reason?
ANGELA 1: So I'd feel sexy.
JACK: Well don't let me inhibit you.
ANGELA 1: I'm trying not to.

TRAVELLING DOWN HER CHILDHOOD GARDEN PATH MEMORY / SIX FOREVER

ANGELA 2: Am I six forever? Six in my thirty-third year. Six sixes are thirty-six. Three and three are six. Six from thirty-three is twenty-seven. Twenty-seven years on a garden path.

Pause.

I'd love a cigarette.

JACK AND ANGELA IN THE KITCHEN /
ABOUT GETTING MARRIED

JACK: Do you want to get married or don't you?

> ANGELA 1 *is not angry here, but she is saying something that hasn't been said before, and perhaps needs to be said, but it is dangerous to say it, so she is careful.*

ANGELA 1: No, we agreed didn't we, I wouldn't marry you, because you couldn't decide to choose just one aspect of life, and murder off all the others.

JACK: It was you who said that to me, before I said it to you.

ANGELA 1: Only because you're such a flirt and I thought I'd better keep up with the Joneses, and get in first.

JACK: Me, a flirt?

> *Slight pause.*

ANGELA 2: Who knows what I might have wanted once before all that from you.

JACK: Maybe we both want something we're pretending we don't.

> *Pause.*

Do you want a cup of tea?

ANGELA 1: Yes I'll have one.

JACK: That's a good sign. Is that a good sign?

ANGELA SITTING / SITTING IN FLESH PINK KITCHEN

As ANGELA 2 *speaks* ANGELA 1 *is not following the words, but she glances sideways to look in the mirror (out towards the audience) and adjust her hair.*

ANGELA 2: My hand lies in my lap. My handbag is on the floor. A lipstick, a comb, a mirror, my car keys, a tissue. My knees are bent slightly sideways, I am twisted in on myself because the tension in my body causes conflict. The wall is a dreadful, flesh pink. If I look a little to the right there's the mirror in which I look at myself every day. I look critically in that mirror. I look for signs. I make an effort to look exactly the same each day. To recognise myself as I was yesterday.

Pause.

There's a picture on the wall of the desert, it looks bare and austere, it looks as if it goes on forever.

We hear the sound of a train as the corridors disappear. Darkness.

SECTION TWO: THE DESERT TRAIN

Throughout this section is an internal monologue to be spoken by ANGELA 1 *from an offstage microphone. It continues (ebbing and flowing) throughout the following section. It is soft and rhythmic.*

ANGELA ON THE TRAIN IN THE DESERT

Upstage we see, as if through an open doorway, an image gradually appear of a desert-scape. The STEWARD *is standing with a tray and cup (a silhouette) in front of the image.* ANGELA 3 *is sitting downstage of the image in a small square of light. There is a slight suggestion of a corridor running from* ANGELA 3 *upstage to the* STEWARD *(low light). As the* STEWARD *moves toward* ANGELA 3, *the image begins to move. We see that it is a view of the desert from the window of a train.* ANGELA 3 *looks towards the audience, as if out the train window.*

ON THE TRAIN

ANGELA 3: With the view out the window, I'm like a baby in a pram…

The STEWARD *appears, with a cup of tea.*

STEWARD: Your tea, madam.
ANGELA 3: Ah. Thank you.

He starts to go.

Could I get something to eat please?

He stops.

STEWARD: You could have a sandwich.

ANGELA 3: A sandwich?

Slight pause.

ANGELA 1'S VOICE: [*voice-over*] Is Jack unconscious…
ANGELA 3: Yes. I'll have a sandwich.

He nods and leaves.

ANGELA 1'S VOICE: [*voice-over*] … kitchen chair, the concrete path, a blue dress, being in school, being in school and the whole world moves, a dining car full of strangers, a desert, have I got a choice? The sound of the train dies down as sleep takes over, I gaze out the window, childhood, a train is like what? Lino on all the floors… A kitchen… Battle of the sexes, cracks in the wall, you're a flirt, no talk, what cannot be said …

ANGELA 3 *looks out the window and drinks some tea.*

LAKE EYRE AND SIMPSON DESERT, SOUTH AUSTRALIA / PART ONE

Through the speaker on the train.

MALE VOICE: [*voice-over*] 'Lake Eyre and the Simpson Desert is the driest part of the Australian continent. Lake Eyre for the most part is a large salt pan at 9,300 square kilometres. The lowest part of Lake Eyre is eleven metres below sea level. Lake Eyre fills a few times each century when the rivers of Queensland receive enough water to push through the dry maze of channels and billabongs on the edge of the Simpson Desert.'

ANGELA *looks out the window.*

ANGELA 3: That's a long wait.

The STEWARD *appears with the sandwich.*

STEWARD: Your sandwich, madam.
ANGELA 1'S VOICE: [*voice-over*] Battle of the sexes, cracks in the wall, you're a flirt …
ANGELA 3: Thank you.

But he has gone. ANGELA *looks at the sandwich then eats it as she looks at the view.*

ANGELA 1'S VOICE: [*voice-over*] …no talk, what cannot be said, are you still sitting there, breathing silence, related to ovulation, dream without words, the kitchen, Jack whistling, they're sunk inside her face, husband and wife, show-off spectacle, fancy dress party, she is here, at the end of the path…

Jack comes in, chops still frozen, got to make a move inside before movement can happen…

THE DEAD HEART

Through the speaker on the train.

MALE VOICE: [*voice-over*] 'The Outback. The Dead Heart. The Desert. These names make you think of images of heat, vast tracts of sand, a featureless wasteland where little grows and nothing lives. Many people think a desert is a desolate and lonely place. But in the desert, by moonlight, animals that are nowhere to be seen during the day, are everywhere.'

ANGELA *looks out the window. The* STEWARD *appears.*

STEWARD: Your cup.
ANGELA 3: Just on the last drop. Then you can have it.
STEWARD: Right.

He slowly starts to go.

ANGELA 3: Excuse me, but could you tell me where we are? Now?
STEWARD: We're on the edge of the Simpson Desert, madam.
ANGELA 3: Oh.

Slight pause.

The dead heart?
STEWARD: [*looking at her*] As you wish.

He goes.

ANGELA 1'S VOICE: [*voice-over*] Jack comes in, chops still frozen, got to make a move inside before movement can happen, girl in kitchen, memory, shadows gradually go, a procession, each one announces themselves with a drum roll, here she comes, birthday girl, I'm no Angel, she gazes across the kitchen, an adult life, a crucial age for a woman, who has not yet fully embarked…

POLAR ICE

Through the speaker on the train.

MALE VOICE: [*voice-over*] 'The desert areas of Australia were once covered by sheets of polar ice and, well before that, by great areas of shallow seas. As our continent edges slowly northwards, its desert regions will have time to reach the equator and once again become tropical regions.'

ANGELA 1'S VOICE: [*voice-over*] … Spring is so evocative, cup of tea and a sandwich, animal instinct, like the horse, she sweeps the path, there is a sandwich in the school bag, no there isn't, blue at night, always at night, little ritual, cup of tea, looking out the window, crying in the distance, mine? Someone else.

MONSOONAL TROUGHS

Through the speaker on the train.

MALE VOICE: [*voice-over*] 'In the Simpson Desert the rainfall is low, but it is not a virtually rainless desert like the Atacama or the Sahara. Even here annual rainfall is hardly below 130 millimetres anywhere.'

ANGELA 1'S VOICE: [*voice-over*] There are always magpies somewhere. A concrete path with grass alongside…

MALE VOICE: [*voice-over*] 'In autumn when monsoonal troughs have penetrated this far south, often it also means floods when three to four years worth of rain come in one fall.'

ANGELA 3: Nothing, nothing, nothing, then a downpour. When it comes it comes.

Slight pause.

STEWARD: Your cup madam.

She hands him the cup and plate.

There will be a stop shortly at Finke River.

ANGELA 3: Can we get out?

STEWARD: Yes. We stop for approximately 45 minutes. You can leave the train, but you must be back on board in plenty of time for departure.

He goes.

16

ANGELA 3: [*calculating*] If I walk for a quarter of an hour to the east then quarter of an hour to the west, I'll make it back in plenty of time.

Blackout and music.

SECTION THREE: IN THE DESERT /
THE DEAD HEART

STAGE 1 : TOTAL DARKNESS

There is total darkness. We hear music. Time passes. We see a small house travelling across the space, in the distance, as if floating. It is internally lit.

STAGE 2 : THE TRAUMA

We hear the sound of ANGELA 1 *laughing in the far, far distance. She is on the edge of hysteria, as one is in childhood (until one is told that's enough now). The laugh becomes deep, sad, lonely, crying.*

Then we see in deep red light, the back of ANGELA 2, *as she stands watching the* GIRL *at some distance from her, struggling as if to assemble or re-assemble her intestines which keep falling out. She is making an enormous effort (it is as if she has ants running all over her body, and time is running out).*

The MOTHER *is standing somewhere else. She is grinding something with a pestle and mortar and her body is moving in the rhythm of the cha cha cha. She is very slow. She keeps falling asleep whilst still standing, her bowl tipping and the powder spilling. The* MOTHER *finally falls to the ground asleep (dead). There is complete silence, and darkness.*

ANGELA 3'S VOICE: Thank God. Everything is decimated.

STAGE 3 : ORIENTATING / I CAN HEAR IT BREATHING

It is still dark, but now the light is strange and optical.

We see all the ANGELAS *in the desert. The* GIRL, *the* MOTHER *and the* FATHER *and* JACK *are also there. They only move slightly at first.* ANGELA *is orientating, coming to terms with the enormity of the space around her, with fear of the dark and the unknown.*

After a while we see ANGELA 3 *sitting on her chair at the side of the space. The light is still very low. We hear her voice murmuring or chanting the following to herself. It is quite distant like a voice inside the wind or nature itself. Gradually the others all leave the space, perhaps walking or crawling away through the trees. The* GIRL *is left lying asleep.*

The FATHER *slowly begins to build the path from a pile of concrete slabs at downstage centre. He is wearing an old suit and felt hat. He taps the edges with a small mallet to make sure they are straight. The path will run from downstage centre to the upstage doorway. He begins at the downstage end of the path which he builds into a small, oblong, paved area. The path will take most of this section to build. At times he stops and rests or thinks or moves somewere else in the space. He takes no notice of the Angelas except perhaps when in relation to the downstage chessboard.*

ANGELA 3: I can hear it breathing, I can hear it, it's moving inside it's moving everywhere, the wind the birds, the air the sky the sun the moon, the stars, the clouds, the grass, the earth, the ants the worms, the spiders, the leaves the trunks, the apples and oranges, the rain the hurricanes the sausages we eat, the potatoes down in the earth, the insects, the darkness, the tree shadows the roots under the ground, the caves, my lunch box my walking, the stillness the winter the hail the snow, little bushes in the desert, the heat rising off the desert the rivers the ponds the puddles, the sea the ocean the moon the stars outer space. The wind, the wind in the sea, the sun in the sand, the rain in the clouds, me in the storm, my body held in the gale rigid forced backwards, the worms down there inside the dry sand, the stars in the sky the hot air in my lungs, the drops of rain down my neck, my back, inside my nose, my mouth, my red blood pumping next to the river.

A redness is beginning to appear in the sky. Complete stillness. We see the GIRL *who is asleep. The light is still low but warming up. Perhaps birds are heard. The* FATHER*'s voice is heard from the distance.*

FATHER: [*voice-over*] Hurry up! Angela! Wake up! Come on, quickly! We'll be late!!

STAGE 4 : THE TRUTH OF THE MATTER

ANGELA 2 *arrives. She is dressed in a nurse's uniform, on the cap is a nightingale feather. She pulls at the* GIRL, *trying to get her to wake and stand. The* GIRL *takes ages to wake, and quite an effort on* ANGELA*'s part to get her up. She finally succeeds. The* FATHER *continues to build the path.*

ANGELA 2: The truth of the matter is that there are two landscapes, Angela. One always on top of the other.

She looks at her watch.

Good timing, the train is in twenty minutes. Come on, there's room at my place, you can stay with me.

Brushing down the GIRL *and tidying her up, she notices the* GIRL*'s legs and stops.*

You've got legs just like mine.

She takes the GIRL *by the hand and walks her upstage to the doorway.*

Don't forget the important things in life. To eat up your greens, to clean your teeth, to look after your health, don't forget to read books, to have friends, to keep up with the world, to bathe frequently.

GIRL'S VOICE: Is it morning yet?

ANGELA 2: Soon.

She picks up a small case and hands it to the GIRL.

Your sandwich, Angela.

ANGELA 2 *disappears off through the trees, singing and speaking to herself.*

Tra-la, la-la-la, tra-la la-la-la…

They built these shoes very well. One could walk anywhere in these. Desert, tarmac, earth, pavement, carpet, sand, grass, and most importantly, for a long time.

The light lifts slightly and the GIRL *looks down and sees ants everywhere.*

GIRL'S VOICE: The ants are everywhere. They're all going somewhere important.

The GIRL *leaves through the upstage doorway.*

STAGE 5 : THE IMPOSSIBLE TASK / ANT NATURE / THE DOMESTIC WORLD IS LAID OUT IN THE DESERT

This section takes place in the domestic areas which are now being laid out in the desert.

The FATHER *continues to build the path.* ANGELA 2, *pulling on her dress, hunts for her keys. She drags a chair from the trees as she hunts.* JACK *carries in a small kitchen table and places it upstage right of the path.*

As the scene proceeds ANGELA 1 *drags the chess table from amongst the downstage left trees and places it in the downstage left position. She works on setting up the table with a chess board and pieces, which she brings from amongst the trees. She is trying, with some difficulty, to remember the position of the pieces of the last game with the mother (perhaps the mother helps her).* ANGELA 3 *watches. And the* GIRL *alternately watches and skips in patterns on the spot. The three Angelas, Jack, the mother, the father and the girl are all involved in this section, but at times we see only one Angela or just Jack and Angela, the other disappearing off into the trees.*

This sequence repeats some of the text from Section One. But the form is changed totally. This is really as a result of new energy and clarity found in the desert. Now there is some space, distance between things, and an ability to feel things physically. There is more of a sense of Angela being 'embodied'. Also it is an older part of Angela, which we now see engaged with Jack.

* *The domestic scenes are now more realistic with some domestic objects being used.*

The GIRL*'s voice is now that of a six-year-old 'found' in the last section. It is spoken by* ANGELA 1.

JACK AND ANGELA IN THE KITCHEN / LATE BREAKFAST AGAIN

ANGELA 2 *is hunting for her keys with real urgency as she's very late for work.* JACK *buttons his shirt.* ANGELA 2 *runs to put on her coat and trips on something.*

ANGELA 2: Where're my keys?!

> JACK *gestures that he doesn't know. She keeps hunting.*

Who left this here?!

> *It is her chair.*

JACK: I think you did. Cup of tea?

> *He hands her tea and picks up a packet of cornflakes.* ANGELA 2, *taking the tea, sips it and burns her tongue.*

ANGELA 2: Oww!

> *She looks at her watch.*

Damn. I hate burning my tongue!

> *She blows on the tea to cool it, then puts it down.*

That hurt!

> *She picks up the cup and continues to drink.* JACK *pours cornflakes into a bowl and out come ants. He leaps up, spilling cornflakes on the floor. He slaps his hands together to squash them.*

JACK: Shit. Now they're in the cornflakes!

> *He looks in the box and bangs it with his hand.* ANGELA 2 *sees her keys on the table and grabs them.*

ANGELA 2: Have to go!

> *She grabs her bag.*

'Bye.

She runs off.

Got to get to work!

ANGELA TRAVELLING DOWN HER CHILDHOOD PATH

GIRL'S VOICE: The mother knocked over the floor
the floor knocked over the kitchen
the kitchen knocked over the door
the door knocked over the path
the path knocked over the schoolgirl
the schoolgirl knocked over the house…

ANGELA 1 *turns to watch the* FATHER *building the path.*

JACK AND ANGELA IN THE KITCHEN / DIRTY DISHES AGAIN

ANGELA 2 *is very pre-menstrual. She suddenly drops her bag and everything falls out. They have just come home from work.* JACK *is drinking milk, chilling out,* ANGELA *is still in momentum.*

ANGELA 2: [*exploding*] Shit!
JACK: What's wrong?
ANGELA 2: I dropped it!
JACK: Slow down.

She stuffs everything back into the bag.

ANGELA 2: Have you done the dishes?
JACK: [*thinking*] I've done them.

Pause.

ANGELA 2: I'm not your mother, Jack.
JACK: I'm sorry.
ANGELA 2: I'm exhausted.

There is a moment of complete stillness.

ANGELA SITTING / BREATHING

ANGELA 3: I can hear it breathing
It's moving… it's moving everywhere.

It's there
it's breathing
it's like…

The previous scene continues with ANGELA 2 *and* JACK. JACK *is trying to lighten things up,*

JACK: I looked after you last night. Didn't I?

Slight pause.

Angel?

ANGELA 2: I'm not an angel.

JACK: Didn't we have a nice time last night?

She grins a little despite herself, but she is trying to stay tough.

ANGELA 2: It's not a joke. I'm serious.

JACK: I'm serious too.

Slight pause.

ANGELA 2: [*not unkindly*] You're unconscious.

JACK *throws it back at her, but with a little humour, not hard.*

JACK: We're all unconscious.

ANGELA TRAVELLING DOWN HER CHILDHOOD PATH

ANGELA 1: One my dad, two my mum, three my cat… one my dad, two my mum, three my cat… one my mum…
Step, step, step, step, step.

ANGELA SITTING / GAPING SPACE

ANGELA 3: My lungs dare to stop
I could die, I do nothing
then a hurricane of air pushes out

emptiness stillness
gaping space.

There is a moment of complete stillness.

JACK AND ANGELA IN THE KITCHEN / ANTS AGAIN

JACK bangs ants on the floor with his foot. ANGELA 1 *flinches.* ANGELA 2 *springs into action when she hears the bang. She has her coat on and her bag, she is ready for work.*

JACK: Ants!
ANGELA 2: It's going to pour.
JACK: You left out the—
ANGELA 2: I know, I know.
JACK: They're all over the place!

> *He's about to have breakfast.*

Did you get the Ant Rid?
ANGELA 2: No. [*Muttering*] That's murder.
JACK: Egh?

> *She starts to go.*

ANGELA 2: I've got to take the car today. Okay?
JACK: Could you give me a lift?
ANGELA 2: Okay.

> *She starts to go.*

But hurry up!
JACK: What about my breakfast?
ANGELA 2: I've got to go now!

> *She starts to go, then stands still.*

ANGELA 3: Right inside my bone is space. And inside my body water.
Water and space.

TRAVELLING DOWN HER CHILDHOOD GARDEN PATH / THE BACKYARD

ANGELA 1: One two, three four five, six.

ANGELA 1 *turns to look at the* GIRL *and the* FATHER, *who is still building the path.*

One two, three four five, six, six today.
I'm six today.

JACK AND ANGELA IN THE KITCHEN / TWO TUNES

ANGELA 2 *is setting up a chess board and pieces, humming her childhood tune which is based on 'one, two, cha cha cha'—'Tra la, la la la'.* JACK *is cleaning up. He stands some distance from* ANGELA 2, *drying a cup. After a little while he starts whistling, his own tune.* ANGELA 2 *continues humming and setting up the chess pieces.* ANGELA 1 *and the* MOTHER *are at the upstage kitchen table.*

ANGELA 2: Tra la, la la la.

She stops.

You always do that!

The GIRL, ANGELA 1 *and the* MOTHER *stop still.*

JACK: What?
ANGELA 2: I was humming a tune.
JACK: Egh?
ANGELA 2: You always come in with another one.

They both go back to their own worlds. Now silent.

ANGELA'S FROZEN SEA DREAM

ANGELA 1 *speaks to the* MOTHER *who is sitting opposite her.*

ANGELA 1: I was swimming under the surface. It was freezing cold, there was ice everywhere. It was really vast, like Alaska or somewhere. A huge sea, but frozen on top. And we had to find cracks or holes in it to be able to come up for breath. It was pretty hard to find any. Then I saw a hole, I grabbed the girl who was behind me. She was nearly drowning. And I pulled her up with me.

She thinks for a moment.

We weren't there yet. But that was the end of the dream.

JACK AND ANGELA IN THE KITCHEN / CHESS

The FATHER *builds another square. The wind is blowing.* JACK *and* AN-GELA 2 *are playing chess.* JACK *moves a piece and takes* ANGELA'*s castle.*

JACK: Ah. Got your castle!
ANGELA 2: Oh no!

> *Pause. She thinks.*

Damn, I wasn't looking that way!

> JACK *watches her for a moment.*

JACK: You could move your—
ANGELA 2: Don't tell me!

> *Slight pause. She stares at the board.*

JACK: Want some wine?
ANGELA 2: Yes, I'll have some.

> JACK *leaves. Pause, stillness.*

MOTHER'S VOICE: Your horse, Angela.

> *Slight pause.*

Use your horse.

> ANGELA 2 *freezes as she hears the* MOTHER'*s voice, and stares at the pieces. Silence.*

ANGELA 3: Obviously the horse does not have a rider
but is an animal
like they say animal instinct

and under them all
checks of black and white
like lino.

ON THE CHILDHOOD PATH

The FATHER *continues to build the path.* ANGELA 1 *is watching the chessboard.*

GIRL'S VOICE: [*humming*] Tra la, la la la, tra la la la la...
ANGELA 3: Two landscapes... on top of each other

Everything
connecting me...

and my imagination
behind it all.

> ANGELA 2 *goes to look in the downstage mirror. She is getting ready for work.*

The solid facts
and my imagination.
My thoughts wandering
going anywhere
connecting me to
it, everywhere...

JACK: [*to* ANGELA 2] Why didn't you dance with me last night?
ANGELA 2: People flirt.

> *Pause.*

You did too.

> ANGELA 2 *moves back up the path and starts practising the cha cha cha.*

ANGELA 3: A part of a picture Angela
just a part
remember that.

Are you big or little?
a dot being fed
or a giant feeding.

Can't see the view
if you're holding the
steering wheel all the time

Angela.

It's not Jack's fault.

JACK AND ANGELA IN THE KITCHEN / THE CHA CHA CHA

ANGELA 2 *is working on her steps, making a connection here with the childhood tune and the chess moves.* JACK *is watching, trying to copy her joining in. During this scene the* FATHER *finishes the path, perhaps completing the last three squares. Then he waits at the downstage end of the path.*

ANGELA 2: Back forward one two three. Forward back cha cha cha!
     Back forward one two three. Forward back cha cha cha!
     Back forward one two three. Forward back cha cha cha!

> JACK *joins in.*

ANGELA 2 & JACK: [*together*] Back forward cha cha cha! Forward back cha cha cha...

JACK: Wow.

ANGELA 2: [*still dancing*] One two, one two three, step step. Step step step...

JACK: When did you learn this?

ANGELA 2: Tra la, la la la, tra la. From my mum.

JACK: It's great!

> JACK *tries to do it, developing it into a dance of his own.* ANGELA 2 *starts to feel tired, stops and watches the amount of energy he still has, her mood shifting to sadness.* JACK *stops and notices her mood. He takes her in his arms. He is now more serious and tender, more adult. After a moment* ANGELA 2 *pulls back and looks at him.*

ANGELA 2: Why don't you do that more often?

JACK: What do you mean?

ANGELA 2: That. Take hold of me like that.

JACK: [*pulling back a little*] Like what?

ANGELA 2: Like that. Like...

JACK: A man.

ANGELA 2: Maybe.

GAME OF CHESS WITH DEAD MOTHER

The MOTHER *is sitting opposite* ANGELA 1 *at the chess table. She is looking a little to the side, not at* ANGELA *or the board. The others all gradually move around the table to watch the chess board.* ANGELA 2 *and* ANGELA 3 *are also looking at the chess board.*

MOTHER'S VOICE: [*voice-over*] It's your move, Angela.

> *Pause.* ANGELA 1 *looks at the* MOTHER'*s face.*

GIRL'S VOICE: Why is your face like that, Mummy?

> *Slight pause.*

It's all yellow.

> *Pause.*

MOTHER'S VOICE: It's not, darling. It must be the light.

> *Pause.*

GIRL'S VOICE: Is Daddy washing the dishes tonight, Mummy?

> *Pause.*

MOTHER'S VOICE: No. He's not home yet.

> *Pause.*

ANGELA 1: Well, who is?

> *Pause.*

MOTHER'S VOICE: No one, darling.

> *Pause.*

It's just you and me tonight.

> *Pause.*

GIRL'S VOICE: But.

> *Pause.*

MOTHER'S VOICE: We'll leave them 'til the morning, sweet.

> *Pause.*

ANGELA 1: It's my birthday, isn't it?

> *Pause.*

I'm six today, aren't I?

Pause.

What do I look like, Mummy?

Pause. The MOTHER *is not looking at her.*

MOTHER'S VOICE: Lovely darling. You are a lovely-looking little girl.

Pause. ANGELA *is realising the* MOTHER *hasn't looked at her.*

You've nothing to worry about.

ANGELA 1: But you didn't look at me.

> *The* MOTHER *leaves. Everyone remains in the same position just looking ahead. There is a hiatus, then* JACK *speaks.*

JACK AND ANGELA IN THE KITCHEN / WINE AND CHIPS

JACK: I'm going to have some wine and chips! Do you want some?

> *No one moves or speaks for a moment.*

ANGELA 2: [*not shifting her focus*] Yes I'll have some.

JACK: That's a good sign. Is that a good sign?

> *They all look at the chess board. There is silence.* ANGELA 1 *picks up her horse and quietly follows the* MOTHER'*s directions.*

ANGELA 2: The horse forward, one, two, one, two three. Check-mate.

> *Pause.*

ANGELA 3: … <u>checked</u> floor, floral dress, very hot…

> *Pause, stillness. The* FATHER *walks up the path and out through the upstage centre exit. The three Angelas listen to his footsteps and remain watching the chess board.*

STAGE 6: THE MEMORIES / TRICK BOX

SCHOOL SHOES

ANGELA 1 *stands and looks at her feet.*

ANGELA 1: I can see my school shoes. They are standing on the floor. In my case is my empty lunch box, the sandwich is chewed up inside my stomach making me sick. It feels like it is trying to push up out of me to throw itself onto the floor.

Slight pause. ANGELA 1 *goes and stands at the top of the path.*

THE FATHER OUTSIDE THE WINDOW

ANGELA 3: Father wasn't sitting in his chair, he was outside, in the backyard.

ANGELA 2 *goes and stands by the side of the trees.*

Walking up and down the path.

Slowly as she sits at the chess table.

And I kept sitting in the house…
in the dark…

THE SOUND OF CICADAS

ANGELA 2: All the time the sound of, cicadas. Then there were the people. There's a long box in front of us.

TRICK BOX / AN HALLUCINATION

ANGELA 1 *moves down the path, stopping halfway down.*

ANGELA 1: It is not what it is, it's a trick box from the circus. My eyes open the lid. X-ray vision eyes.

She is in her best dress, her head, her hair, her calm face. I know she's in there. She's sleeping beauty, about to be cut in two. I know it's a trick. The man has his enormous hacksaw. Under the lid her stomach is inside her dress. He is sawing. Flesh rips and blood spurts. The poor princess screams bloody murder. Something has gone wrong, something has gone wrong, something has gone wrong. All the forests are falling, the saw is screaming, it is hacking at the wood, hacking at the flesh. The prince is hacking at the brambles. The box is falling apart, nothing.

Slight pause.

Where is she? Where is she?

ANGELA DOWN THE THROAT

The MOTHER, *without mask, appears and begins to walk slowly down the path. She reaches the bottom of the path and then lies down across the end of it. During the following speech the* GIRL *slowly walks down the path.*

ANGELA 2: It's a highway. A super highway. I'll go down the left side and back up the right. I'll meet a trap door somewhere down here. On the other side pink landscape, mountains, hills, valleys, a sky of pink. I can feel my panic. A wind, flattening me. I'll cling to the sides. I'm slipping. It's dark, a red door. I'm in a chamber.
A red chamber, a word is moving up over my tongue…

The GIRL *stands looking down at the* MOTHER.

E – mo – shun, e – motion,
emotion emotion emotion emotion…

Everyone disappears as we hear the sound of the train. Blackout.

SECTION FOUR: THE DESERT TRAIN / DINING CAR

ANGELA ON THE TRAIN / THE RETURN JOURNEY

All of the ANGELAS *and the* MAN *are sitting along the path. The waiter stands at the end of the path with a tray.*

It is night. The train is on the last lap of its journey, travelling through the desert, towards town. Perhaps there are small lights on in the dining car, and travelling around the circumference of the set. The atmosphere is one of tremendous release and social and sexual boldness. ANGELA *is fantasising or practicing re-entering the social world here, she is putting herself back together. The night is shooting past. The feeling is warm and luminous. There are no real props, just the* WAITER.

WAITER: The menu, madam.

ANGELA 1: Thank you.

ANGELA 3: I'd like a glass of dry white.

MAN: I'd like a chardonnay!

ANGELA 1: Me too!

WAITER: Very good, madam.

ANGELA 2: I'd like one too.

WAITER: Certainly, madam.

ANGELA 1: God I'm starving.

ANGELA 3: Perhaps I'll have a large, juicy, rare steak.

MAN: The fish looks delicious!

ANGELA 1: To sum it all up life will go on.

ANGELA 3: Or not.

WAITER: Would you care to order now, madam?

ANGELA 2: Ah yes. I'll have the fish…

ANGELA 3: …and salad…

ANGELA 1: …and then the strawberries.

WAITER: Very good, madam.

ANGELA 3: I'd like some crusty bread, perhaps with poppy seeds.

MAN: I really fancy a big, juicy steak.

ANGELA 2: You're such a carnivore!

WAITER: Excuse me madam. Your fish.

ANGELA 1: Oh. Thank you.

ALL ANGELAS: Mmm, delicious!

ANGELA 3: It's so good to be cooked for!

ANGELA 1: I wouldn't miss out on any of it, for the world.

WAITER: Any one want filling it?

ALL: Me, I do! I do!!

WAITER: That's a nice scent. Now what is the name of that?

ANGELA 3: Calvin Klein, Male and Female.

WAITER: Oh!

ANGELA 3: A creative combination.

WAITER: [laughing] I must get some.

ANGELA 3: Helps solve problems.

WAITER: Goodness!

MAN: Have you got any OJ?

ANGELA 1: Who does the housework at your place?

MAN: We do exactly half each. And fair enough too!

WAITER: OJ? We certainly do, sir!

ANGELA 2: Housework, who cares, what a bore, I hate it.

ANGELA 3: You have to live your own life, you can't live your life through your children.

WAITER: *Your strawberries, madam.*

ANGELA 1: *Mmmmm!*

WAITER: *Another glass of wine, madam?*

ANGELA 1: *Oh. Yes thank you!*

> *He leans over and pours the wine.*

WAITER: *And may I ask if it was the cream or the ice cream with the strawberries?*

ALL: *Oh... The cream! Thank you.*

MAN: Make your bed and then lie in it, I say.

ANGELA 1: I don't believe that.

WAITER: And whose was the chicken?

MAN: Not mine.

ANGELA 2: I'm determined to go with the flow.

MAN: Determined? That's not a contradiction in terms is it?

ANGELA 3: I'll have to have a think about that. Oh me! I'm the chicken! Or was I the fish?

ANGELA 1: I stood on a chicken by mistake when I was little.

ALL: Ugh!

MAN: You stood on a chicken!

ANGELA 1: What about revolutionaries, what about change, that sort of thing.

MAN: Well I wouldn't have my life any other way.

ANGELA 2: I love change. I change around the furniture all the time.

ANGELA 1: You've gone quiet. What're you thinking?

ANGELA 3: Not many would have any idea how old I am.

WAITER: A top up, madam?

> *ANGELA 2 addresses everyone on the train.*

ANGELA 2: *His body hung in space like sexual atmosphere, you couldn't help ingest him and even if his mind was elsewhere, he knew he was disappearing down your gullet and up your cunt!*

MAN: And who was he!

ANGELA 1: He was the Animus!

MAN: Oh. I see.

ANGELA 2: Oh no, I've spilt the wine! It's all over the floor.
WAITER: Not to worry! I'll fix it, ma'am.
ANGELA 3: If you have sex in a dream is that betrayal?
MAN: That depends. I'll have to think about that.
ANGELA 1: It's no good saying I wish, you have to act, I say.
ANGELA 2: Well I act all the time.
ANGELA 3: We all act.
MAN: Well I must say I love the way you do it.
ANGELA 1: She's inside her own erotic rhythm, that's the trick!

She laughs.

MAN: Really.
ANGELA 1: Yes!
MAN: Very impressive.
ANGELA 3: Thank you. I adore positive feedback!
WAITER: Can I fill you up again, ma'am?
ANGELA 2: You can fill me up again any time you like!
ANGELA 1: She's using up life. That's what is so admirable.
WAITER: Very good, ma'am. I'm at your service!
MAN: I've decided! The dream. It can't possibly be betrayal!
ANGELA 1: That's just as well.
ANGELA 3: Let's plan something. An adventure. We need something
    unexpected. Something exciting.
ANGELA 2: An event.
ANGELA 1: Or something noticeable at least!

*ANGELA 2 looks to window and begins to wipe some cream off her
lips, the WAITER speaks, everyone listens in.*

WAITER: *Could I lick that cream off your lips.*
ANGELA 2: *Maybe you could.*
WAITER: *I've imagined doing it. Or something like it.*
ANGELA 2: *Have you…?*
WAITER: *Herman.*

They look at each other for a moment.

ANGELA 2: *Well, Herman, I'd like to know what the something like it was!*
WAITER: *I'll see what I can do!*

MAN: Now just look at that moon.
ANGELA 1: I adore the sky, don't you?

MAN: The enormity of it all.

ANGELA 3: I've decided, hell is resistance.

WAITER: Are you ready for coffee, ma'am?

ANGELA 2: In a minute, just filling the tank.

ANGELA 3: I'm a mature woman. I have no desire to go backwards. I adore adventure!

ANGELA 1: I'd like a large glass of water please, waiter.

WAITER: Of course, right away, ma'am.

ALL ANGELAS: Oh, I'd like one too!! Me too!

WAITER: I'll be right back.

MAN: I'll have some more of that too!

ANGELA 2: I thought fancy dress would be the thing.

ANGELA 3: Whoops! I nearly knocked my glass over!

MAN: What a great idea for a birthday.

ANGELA 1: I'll bet she's procrastinating.

ANGELA 2: The point is, you can be anybody you like!

ANGELA 3: And still be yourself.

MAN: How old is she turning?

ANGELA 2: I think she thinks it's a delicate age.

ANGELA 3: Well it's all psychological.

ANGELA 1: Well I'm sick of hearing that! I think things are physical.

MAN: Well, that's precisely why I jog!

WAITER: Now anyone for a last coffee before we arrive?

ANGELA 3: [she gets a fright] Oh! I was miles away!

WAITER: Coffee, madam?

ANGELA 3: Thank you.

SECTION FIVE: THE TUMBLEWEED SONG

We see the WAITER *singing, perhaps at a downstage microphone.* ANGELA *3 packs away the chess pieces and board, and drinks her coffee.*

At the back of the stage we see a repeat of the image from Section Two. The image is once again out the window of the train, but now the train is passing the outer suburbs of Adelaide. We see backyards sliding past. Until it comes to a stop at the end of the film outside a suburban backyard.

TUMBLEWEED SONG

WAITER: [*singing*]

She's an angel
from the dark of the night,
She's an angel,
but she says she's not,

From the desert on the wind
she's rolled,
rolled right back in.
But she's on the move now,
She says, she's on the move.

She's an angel
from the dark of the night,
She's an angel
but she says she's not

From the desert,
a tumble weed.
She's on the move now,
she'll keep on rolling
on the wind.

She's an angel
from the dark of the night,
She's an angel,
but she says she's not,

From the desert,
a tumble weed.
She's on the move now,
she'll keep on rolling
on the wind.

SECTION SIX: ANGELA AND OTTO

ANGELA AND OTTO / THE VISIT

This scene should be quite realistically played. ANGELA 3 *is sitting in her kitchen. The scene could be a fantasy or an actual meeting with Otto. In any case it has the feeling of either and both of these scenarios. It should be quite charged—these two have not seen each other for many years and suddenly he has rung and asked if he could pop in. They have interesting chemistry.* OTTO *is standing on the other side of the table.*

ANGELA 3: You look as if you have come through a thunderstorm.
OTTO: No across a desert.

> *She laughs.*

Really I've just come across the desert.
ANGELA 3: Oh. You won't believe this but so have I.
OTTO: Really?
ANGELA 3: Amazing!

> *Pause.*

OTTO: It's so relentless driving through the desert, you feel like it'll never stop. I like that.
ANGELA 3: Me too.

> *They smile and relax.*

Why are you here?
OTTO: I don't know many people on this side of Australia.

> *Pause.*

I know you.
ANGELA 3: You don't really.
OTTO: That's true.
ANGELA 3: Well here I am.

> *They look at each other.*

OTTO: Can I get a glass of water? And make some toast? I've got some bread in the car.

ANGELA 3: Should be things in the fridge. In the Kelvinator. It's very domestic here I would imagine, coming off the desert, to find me and a kitchen.

OTTO: You're different.

Pause.

ANGELA 3: How're your children?

OTTO: Really good.

ANGELA 3: That's good.

OTTO: You haven't got any?

ANGELA 3: No.

OTTO: Not yet?

ANGELA 3: No.

Pause.

I haven't had a good time lately.

Pause.

OTTO: What's wrong?

ANGELA 3: Probably grief.

Slight pause.

In a way.

Pause.

OTTO: Would you like a drink? I've brought a bottle.

ANGELA 3: That'd be nice.

OTTO: I might see if I can find some work over here.

ANGELA 3: You're going to stay?

OTTO: I thought I might.

ANGELA 3: Oh. And the family?

OTTO: Well, they're over there.

ANGELA 3: Oh.

OTTO: It's really nice to see you.

ANGELA 3: It's my birthday soon. I'm supposed to be having a party. Here. You can come if you like. Maybe fancy dress.

OTTO: [*smiling*] I'd like to do that.

OTTO *disappears.*

SECTION SEVEN: THE BIRTHDAY PARTY—WHY WAS SHE BORN AT ALL?!

The birthday party is both real and in the imagination. The following could be sung.

All the characters are on the path. The scene may take a while to establish. They are moving as a group from one end of the path to the other, swapping places, circling around each other. Their movements are particular and interesting. They all dance their way up and down the path and through various stages of dance.

THE FANCY DRESS ROLL CALL

THE GRAVEDIGGER: To Angela Queen of the Tumbleweed!! Hooray!!
  Hooray for Queen of the Tumbleweed! Hooray!
  To the Shakespearean grave digger from…?!
  Hamlet! Hooray! 'In youth when I did love, did love!!'
  A thirty-three-year-old schoolgirl!
  Hip, hip, hooray!
  To perseverance! Hooray!
  A witch, from out of the ditch!
  Hooray! Hooray!
  A Shakespearean character who is one gender but appears as another?
  To Rosalind!!
  Proof, proof. Let's have proof!

  ANGELA 1 *strips her top half revealing a sexy bra.*

  Ooooh!! Ahhhh!! Owooo! Sexy!
  To one whose name's almost right!
  If you take it in flight!
  Hooray!
  Hermes! The god of safe travel!
  To trains! To the Ghan!!! To camel trains!
  Hooray!
  A creature that sleeps in the day and wakes in the night?

That's blind, and hangs upside down!
Hooray for the bat!
Hooray for bats!
Hooray for newborns!
To all newborns!!
A cross between a nurse and a bird?
Florence Nightingale!!
To The Ant! To Ant Nature!
Hooray!
To An–gel–ah! Angel fish! Angel cake! To Angel Cake!
Hooray! No egg yokes!
Hooray!!
Hooray for Eggs!
To Angel! 'I'm not an Angel!'
Hooray!!
To the earthling!

SECTION EIGHT: BACK HOME WITH THE DESERT IN-SIDE

SITTING ANGELA / WITH THE DESERT INSIDE

ANGELA 3: Outside me is the night
    sky the universe
    the big picture

    on the train
    past the trees
    past the hills
    into the desert
    past oceans of landscape
    into the suburbs
    the backyards
    the backyard
    the house
    the rooms
    the floors the walls

chairs tables
the people
then back out again
out the window
up out into
nowhere
everywhere

the ant
the horse
the human

THE END